W9-ACR-765

from SEA TO SHINING SEA

Rhode Island

By Dennis Brindell Fradin and Judith Bloom Fradin

CONSULTANTS

Albert T. Klyberg, Director of the Rhode Island Historical Society

Robert L. Hillerich, Ph.D., Professor Emeritus, Bowling Green State University;
Consultant, Pinellas County Schools, Florida

CHILDRENS PRESS®

CHICAGO

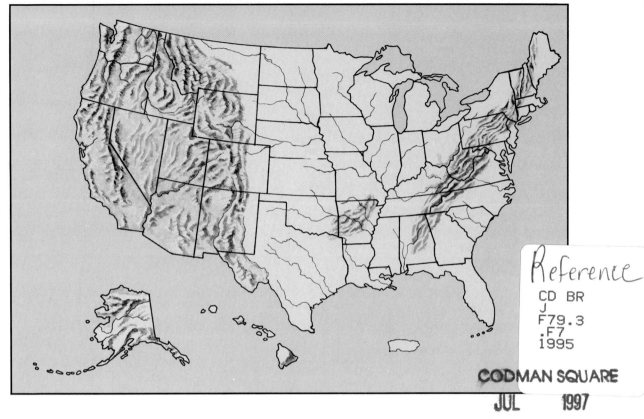

Reference
CD BR
J
F79.3
.F7
1995

CODMAN SQUARE

JUL   1997

Rhode Island is one of the six states in the region called New England. The other New England states are Connecticut, Maine, Massachusetts, New Hampshire, and Vermont.

For our dear friend, Anthony Wallace

Front cover picture: Southeast Lighthouse, Block Island; page 1: The start of a Newport sailing race; back cover: Thomas Street, Providence

Project Editor: Joan Downing
Design Director: Karen Kohn
Research Assistant: Lori Fradin
Typesetting: Graphic Connections, Inc.
Engraving: Liberty Photoengraving

Copyright © 1995 Childrens Press®, Inc.
All rights reserved. Published simultaneously in Canada.
Printed in the United States of America.
1 2 3 4 5 6 7 8 9 10 R 04 03 02 01 00 99 98 97 96 95

Library of Congress Cataloging-in-Publication Data

Fradin, Dennis B.
  Rhode Island / by Dennis Brindell Fradin & Judith
Bloom Fradin.
    p.   cm. — (From sea to shining sea)
  Includes index.
  ISBN 0-516-03839-7
  1. Rhode Island—Juvenile literature. I. Fradin, Judith
Bloom. II. Title. III. Series: Fradin, Dennis B. From sea
to shining sea.
F79.3.F7   1995   95-18800
974.5—dc20   CIP
                                                  AC

Table of Contents

Face painting at the Providence Waterfront Festival

INTRODUCING THE OCEAN STATE

Rhode Island is in the northeastern United States. It lies along the Atlantic Ocean. Its main nickname is the "Ocean State." Rhode Island is the smallest of the fifty states. Another nickname is "Little Rhody." Rhode Islanders are proud of their state. "The smallest state," says the state song, "and yet so great."

Rhode Island was one of England's thirteen colonies. It allowed religious freedom to all who lived there. Later, Rhode Island became one of the original thirteen states. The state also was a business leader. America's first machine-run cotton mill was built in Pawtucket.

Today, Rhode Islanders are known as jewelry and silverware makers. They also make boats and ships. Each year, visitors enjoy Rhode Island's seaside resorts and interesting towns.

The Ocean State is known for much more. Which colony first dropped allegiance to the King of England? Where were teacher Prudence Crandall and artist Gilbert Stuart born? Where is the country's oldest Jewish synagogue? The answer to these questions is: Rhode Island!

*A picture map
of Rhode Island*

*Overleaf: Boulders at
Mohegan Bluffs, Block
Island*

5

Coastlands, Islands, and Woodlands

Coastlands, Islands, and Woodlands

Rhode Island covers 1,212 square miles. It is part of New England. Two other New England states border Rhode Island. Massachusetts is to the east and north. Connecticut is to the west. The Atlantic Ocean is south of Rhode Island. Narragansett Bay is an arm of the Atlantic. It reaches deep within eastern Rhode Island.

Thirty-six islands are also part of the state. The largest is 45-square-mile Aquidneck Island. It's in Narragansett Bay. Block Island lies offshore. It's in the Atlantic Ocean.

The state's lowest point is sea level, along the coast. The Ocean State has no mountains. However, it does have sea cliffs and hills. Jerimoth Hill is Rhode Island's highest point. It's in northeast Rhode Island. This hill is 812 feet above sea level.

Block Island coastline

Waters, Woods, and Wildlife

No place in Rhode Island is far from water. The state has a 384-mile coastline. That's counting the seacoast and all the bays and islands. Within the

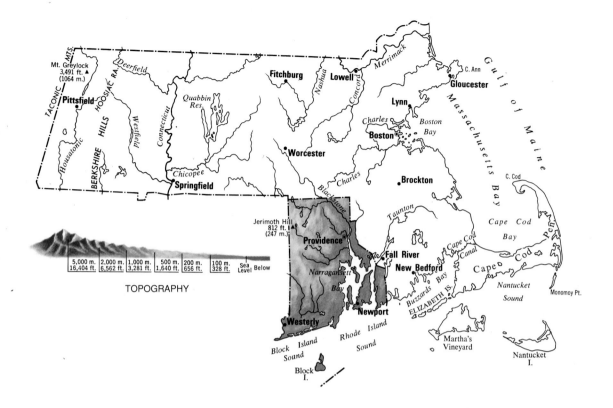

Mt. Greylock
3,491 ft. ▲
(1064 m.)

TACONIC MTS.

Pittsfield

Deerfield

HOOSAC RA.

BERKSHIRE HILLS

Housatonic

Westfield

Connecticut

Quabbin Res.

Fitchburg

Lowell

Nashua

Concord

Merrimack

C. Ann

Gloucester

Lynn

Charles

Boston Bay

Boston

Gulf of Maine

Massachusetts Bay

Chicopee

Springfield

Worcester

Charles

Blackstone

Brockton

Taunton

C. Cod

Cape Cod Bay

Jerimoth Hill
812 ft.
(247 m.)

Providence

Fall River

New Bedford

Cape Cod Canal

Cape Cod

Narragansett Bay

Buzzards Bay

ELIZABETH IS.

Nantucket Sound

Monomoy Pt.

Newport

Westerly

Block Island Sound

Rhode Island Sound

Martha's Vineyard

Nantucket I.

Block I.

5,000 m.
16,404 ft. | 2,000 m.
6,562 ft. | 1,000 m.
3,281 ft. | 500 m.
1,640 ft. | 200 m.
656 ft. | 100 m.
328 ft. | Sea Level | Below

TOPOGRAPHY

state are nearly 300 lakes and ponds. Scituate Reservoir is Rhode Island's largest lake. It was formed by a dam built on the Pawtuxet River. Other Rhode Island rivers are the Blackstone, Woonasquatucket, Chepachet, and Wood.

Woodlands cover about three-fifths of Rhode Island. The red maple is the state tree. Oaks, ashes, birches, elms, hemlocks, and poplars are other Rhode Island trees. Shrubs, or small trees, called pussy willows grow there, too. Jamestown has the country's second-largest pussy willow. Michigan has the biggest one. Many wildflowers also grow in the Ocean State. The violet is the state flower.

9

White-tailed deer roam Rhode Island. So do foxes, woodchucks, rabbits, minks, and raccoons. Gulls, ducks, pheasants, owls, and catbirds fly over the land and water. Whales swim off Rhode Island's coast. The quahog is a kind of clam. Its shell is the state shell.

CLIMATE

For a place so far north, Rhode Island has mild weather. Breezes from the ocean and Narragansett Bay cool the state in summer. They warm it in winter. Summer temperatures often rise above 70

Left: White-tailed deer, a doe and her fawn
Right: Wild buttercups

degrees Fahrenheit. The thermometer often tops 35 degrees Fahrenheit on winter days. Rhode Island's rain and melted snow amount to about 44 inches each year. The state receives about 30 inches of snow a year.

Hurricanes sometime strike the state. These strong windstorms start over the ocean. They do great damage when they hit land. In 1938, the New England Hurricane struck. Rhode Island received the most damage. More than 300 Rhode Islanders were killed. Over $100 million in damage was done. Hurricane Bob caused over $115 million in damage in 1991.

An aerial view of Block Island in winter

The 1938 New England Hurricane killed about 600 people throughout New England.

11

From Ancient Times Until Today

From Ancient Times Until Today

About 2 million years ago, the Ice Age began. Glaciers covered Rhode Island. These huge ice sheets slowly moved over the land. They carved holes in it. About 10,000 years ago, the glaciers melted. The melting ice formed many lakes and ponds.

Native Americans

The first people reached Rhode Island at least 8,000 years ago. These early Rhode Islanders hunted deer with spears. They gathered clams along Narragansett Bay.

By the year 1500, several Indian groups lived in Rhode Island. The Narragansetts were Rhode Island's largest group. The Wampanoags, Niantics, Nipmucs, and Pequots were other groups. The Indians lived in round huts called wigwams. For water travel, they used canoes. Indian women grew the village's corn, squash, and beans. The men brought home deer and fish to eat.

The Indians made beads from shells. The beads were called wampum. Wampum was used as money.

Opposite: The Pawtuxet Rangers of the Rhode Island Militia participate in a Barrington Memorial Day parade.

13

Wampum beads were also strung together to make pictures. The pictures were used in messages. They also told the Indians' history.

EUROPEAN EXPLORERS

Giovanni da Verrazano was Rhode Island's first known European visitor. He was an Italian sailing for the French. In 1524, Verrazano explored Narragansett Bay. One of the islands reminded him of the island of Rhodes. That's near Greece. This may have been how Rhode Island got its name.

Dutch people live in the Netherlands.

In 1614, Adriaen Block sailed along Rhode Island's shore. He was a Dutch explorer. Block named a nearby island *Roodt Eylandt.* That means "Red Island" in Dutch. The island had red clay along its shore. Over time, the name may have become *Rhode Island.* Today, that island is called Block Island. It was named for Adriaen Block.

COLONIAL RHODE ISLAND

England began settling colonies in North America during the 1600s. The first colonists reached Massachusetts in 1620. People who lived in Massachusetts had to hold certain religious views. If they didn't,

Massachusetts' government sent them away. In 1635, William Blackstone left Massachusetts partly over religion. He built a farm called Study Hill. That was near present-day Cumberland, Rhode Island. There, he spent his time gardening and reading. Blackstone was Rhode Island's first settler. But he did not set up a colony.

The Blackstone River was named for William Blackstone.

Roger Williams was a minister in Massachusetts. He taught that government should be separate from religion. Massachusetts leaders ordered his arrest. In 1636, Williams and a few friends escaped to Rhode Island. They bought land from the Wampanoag and Narragansett Indians. Williams then founded Provi-

When Roger Williams landed in Rhode Island, he was greeted warmly by Wampanoag Indians.

dence. This was Rhode Island's first non-Indian town. Its name means "God's watchful care." Providence offered religious freedom to all. It was America's first town to do that.

Anne Hutchinson was also charged with holding wrong religious views. Besides, she had been preaching. That was said to be a man's job. Hutchinson and others left Massachusetts. They founded Portsmouth in 1638. People with other religious views founded other towns. Newport was settled in 1639. Warwick was begun in 1642. These colonists also bought Indian land for their towns.

In 1644, Roger Williams received a grant from England. It allowed the four towns to form a colony. Williams was Rhode Island's first governor. Rhode Island's constitution said that government and religion would be separate there.

People of many faiths came to the little colony. They included Quakers and Jews. The other colonies called Rhode Island "Rogue Island." They didn't think Rhode Island should open its door to everyone. Today, Rhode Island is known as the birthplace of religious freedom in America.

Roger Williams had always treated the Indians fairly. People in other colonies grabbed Indian lands. Metacomet, the Wampanoag chief, struck back. In

The Quaker Meeting House in Little Compton

King Philip's War (1675-1676), the Wampanoags and Narragansetts fought New Englanders. King Philip was the colonists' name for Metacomet. About 1,000 Indians were killed at the Great Swamp Fight. That happened in southern Rhode Island in December 1675. Metacomet was killed in 1676. The war ended soon after.

The colonists attacked the Narragansett fort during King Philip's War.

Rhode Island remained an English colony until 1776. During that time, more new towns were begun. By 1720, 12,000 settlers lived in Rhode Island. Most of them farmed. Others worked as sailors or built ships. The shipping business also became important. Many Rhode Island merchants grew rich from it. Some of them entered the slave trade. Ships built in Rhode Island brought 90 percent of all slaves to the colonies. Newport had the largest number of slaves in New England. In 1774, Rhode Island outlawed the bringing in of slaves. It was the first colony to do that.

THE REVOLUTIONARY WAR

In the 1760s, England began taxing the colonists heavily. By this time, there were thirteen English colonies. Some colonists, called patriots, struck back. In 1769, Rhode Island patriots burned the

Rhode Island patriots set the English ship Gaspee *on fire in 1772.*

English ship *Liberty* at Newport. In 1772, near Providence, they set the English ship *Gaspee* on fire. In 1774, the thirteen colonies banded together. In 1775, the Revolutionary War started.

On May 4, 1776, Rhode Island stopped its allegiance to the King of England. It was the first colony to do that. That July 4, American leaders approved the Declaration of Independence. It said that the colonies were now the United States. Two Rhode Islanders signed the Declaration of Independence. They were Stephen Hopkins and William Ellery.

Stephen Hopkins helped create the new country's navy. His brother, Esek Hopkins, led it. Nathanael Greene from Warwick was a great general in the war. About 10,000 other Rhode Islanders also fought England. The Battle of Rhode Island was the state's biggest battle. It occurred at Portsmouth and Newport in August 1778. Rhode Island soldiers who were former slaves held off three enemy charges. The English stayed in Newport, however, until 1779. The Revolutionary War ended in 1783. The United States had won its freedom.

THE THIRTEENTH STATE

In 1787, leaders from twelve states wrote the United States Constitution. This set up the country's government. Rhode Island did not take part. Its leaders feared that the big states would run the new government. Rhode Islanders wanted the Constitution to have a bill of rights. That would protect people's major rights. By 1790, Congress was working on the Bill of Rights. That May 29, Rhode Island leaders approved the Constitution. Little Rhody became the thirteenth state.

Shipbuilding and shipping remained important in the young state. Other industries quickly grew in

Nathanael Green

19

Rhode Island. Rhode Island became the country's jewelry-making center. Silverware, guns, and candles were other goods made there. By 1795, clothmaking became the state's most important business.

By the late 1700s, cloth was still made by hand in the United States. England had water-powered machines to do the job. But the plans for these machines were kept secret. Samuel Slater worked in an English cotton factory. He knew how water-

Cotton being spun into yarn at an early Rhode Island cotton mill

driven machines should work. Slater came to America and in 1790 went to work for Moses Brown at Pawtucket. Together, they set up the country's first water-powered cotton mill. Soon Slater and others opened their own mills.

Thousands of people came to Rhode Island. Many were from Ireland, Canada, Sweden, Germany, and Portugal. They made cloth in the state's many mills. Big cities grew around the mills.

Rhode Island's factory workers weren't allowed to vote. Only landowners could do that. More people lived in Rhode Island's cities than in small towns. Yet, small towns had more lawmakers in the state legislature. Thomas Dorr tried to change this. He was a Rhode Island lawyer. In 1842, Dorr formed an army. He tried to replace the state government with a fairer one. The "Dorr Rebellion" was squashed. Dorr was jailed. But Rhode Island wrote a new constitution in late 1842. It allowed more people to vote. The cities also gained more representatives. This constitution still guides Rhode Island today.

Thomas Dorr

Rhode Island had outlawed slavery in 1784. By 1820, it was outlawed in the other northern states. The southern states still allowed slavery. Many anti-slavery meetings were held in Providence. Rhode

Islanders also hid southern slaves who were escaping to Canada. One such hiding place was Elizabeth Buffum Chace's house.

The Civil War (1861-1865) ended the fight about slavery. This war was between the northern states and the southern states. Rhode Island sent 24,000 soldiers and sailors to serve the North. They included 2,000 black troops. Ambrose Burnside, a northern general, was from Rhode Island. The North won the war in 1865. Slavery ended in the United States.

GROWTH, WORLD WARS, AND DEPRESSION

In the late 1800s, Rhode Island's textile industry grew. So did the jewelry and silverware businesses. More Europeans moved to Rhode Island. They came from Italy, Poland, Russia, and Greece. Between 1900 and 1910, the population rose from 429,000 to 543,000. This was the state's biggest ten-year growth.

Newport became a vacation center in the late 1800s. Big summer homes were built there. Wealthy Newporters spent up to $300,000 during a single summer. Newport also became a sports center. In 1881, Newport hosted the first United States

Elizabeth Chace

national lawn tennis championship. The first United States amateur golf championship was held there in 1895. In 1883, the Newport Naval Station was built.

The United States entered World War I (1914-1918) in 1917. Rhode Island provided warships and weapons. About 28,000 Rhode Islanders served in uniform.

Soon after the war was won, trouble struck at home. In the 1920s, many clothmaking companies left Rhode Island. They moved to the South where workers were paid less. To make things worse, the Great Depression (1929-1939) hit the country. Fac-

Immigrants from Europe added to Rhode Island's population in the early 1900s.

tories and banks closed. Many other Rhode Islanders lost their jobs.

World War II (1939-1945) helped end the depression. The United States entered the war in 1941. Rhode Island factories swung into gear for the war. They made ships and torpedoes. At Quonset Point, workers built lightweight sheet-metal buildings. These Quonset huts were used as hospitals. Soldiers lived in them, too. Nearly 100,000 Rhode Islanders in uniform helped win the war.

RECENT GROWTH AND CHANGES

In the 1950s, new industries became important in Rhode Island. Companies that made chemicals, machinery, and electronics came to the state. Banking grew. So did health care and government work.

Transportation improved, too. In 1969, the Newport Bridge was finished over Narragansett Bay. It connects Newport with Conanicut Island. More hotels and resorts have been built throughout the state. Also in 1969, Interstate 95 was completed. This connects Rhode Island with Connecticut and Massachusetts. In the 1980s, many people from the Boston, Massachusetts, area moved to Rhode Island. Each day, they travel to work in Boston.

Boston, Massachusetts, is only about 30 miles from Rhode Island.

Rhode Island also faces some problems. The jewelry-making business has gone down. Many navy bases have been closed. Rhode Island's jobless rate has gone up. In 1991, a banking crisis hit the state. It forced forty-five Rhode Island banks and credit unions to close. Thirteen of them never reopened. Providence has many overcrowded schools. Classes sometimes meet in churches and YMCAs.

On the brighter side, Narragansett Bay is being cleaned up. Today, eight-tenths of the bay's pollution is gone. This has been done through a citizens' group called Save the Bay. Rhode Islanders want to save and improve upon the Ocean State's beauty.

Newport Bridge

Overleaf: A girl learning to sail at Newport

Rhode Islanders and Their Work

RHODE ISLANDERS AND THEIR WORK

Little Rhody has just over 1 million people. The state ranks forty-third in population. Nine-tenths of Rhode Islanders live in or near cities. They also live rather close together. The Ocean State has almost 1,000 people per square mile. Only New Jersey is more crowded.

Rhode Island has many kinds of people. Nine-tenths of them are white. Many of them have Irish, Italian, English, French, or Portuguese backgrounds. Rhode Island has about 50,000 Hispanic (Spanish-speaking) people. Many of them came from the Dominican Republic or Puerto Rico. About 40,000 Rhode Islanders are black. Another 20,000 are Asian-Americans. Less than 5,000 are American Indians. The Narragansetts are the biggest Indian group. They have about 2,000 people.

Alaska, the least-crowded state, has one person per square mile. So the smallest state is one thousand times as crowded as the largest state.

Children sitting on the State House steps in Providence

RHODE ISLANDERS AT WORK

Nearly 500,000 Rhode Islanders have jobs. Service work is the leading kind of job. The state has nearly 150,000 service workers. They are computer and car repairers, lawyers, doctors, and nurses.

27

Selling goods is the second-leading kind of work. Nearly 100,000 Rhode Islanders sell goods. These goods range from cars to diamond rings. About 90,000 Rhode Islanders make goods. Jewelry and silverware are leading products. Only New York is ahead of Rhode Island at making these things. Other metal goods are also made in Rhode Island. They include nuts, bolts, and pipe fittings. The state is a center for building and repairing boats. Pawtucket is the home of Hasbro, Inc. This is a giant toy company. They make Playskool toys, G.I. Joe action figures, Mr. Potato Head, and other toys.

Government work employs 60,000 people. Many of them work in public schools. The navy is a big Rhode Island employer, too. There are still

Left: A Brown University student Right: A man and woman in costume for the Bristol July Fourth celebration

some navy bases along Narragansett Bay. And the Naval War College employs many people. Over 25,000 Rhode Islanders work in banking and connected fields. A major banking company is Citizens Bank. It is based in Providence.

About 6,000 Rhode Islanders farm or fish. Nursery plants are the top farm product. They include sod, trees, and shrubs. Milk, potatoes, apples, hay, and chickens are other farm goods. The Rhode Island Red is a kind of chicken. Its meat tastes good. It lays large eggs. The Rhode Island Red is the state bird. Rhode Island fishermen bring back flounder, tuna, lobsters, and clams. Little Rhody has few miners. Stone and sand and gravel are the top mining goods.

The Naval War College in Newport

Overleaf: Misquamicut State Beach, Block Island Sound

An Ocean State Tour

AN OCEAN STATE TOUR

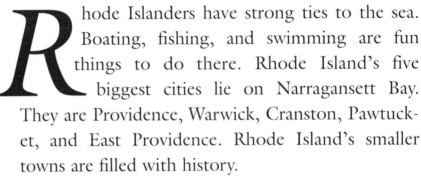

Rhode Islanders have strong ties to the sea. Boating, fishing, and swimming are fun things to do there. Rhode Island's five biggest cities lie on Narragansett Bay. They are Providence, Warwick, Cranston, Pawtucket, and East Providence. Rhode Island's smaller towns are filled with history.

PROVIDENCE

Providence is a good place to start a trip around the Ocean State. This is the state's biggest city. More than 160,000 people live there. Providence is also one of the oldest cities in the United States. It was founded by Roger Williams in 1636.

Roger Williams National Memorial marks where the town began. Visitors can learn about the "Father of Rhode Island" there. The Meeting House of the First Baptist Church in America is nearby. The country's oldest Baptist congregation meets there. Roger Williams began it in 1639. The First Unitarian Church is another landmark. Paul Revere's company made its steeple bell in 1816.

The First Baptist Church in Providence was begun by Roger Williams in 1639.

Roger Williams Park is in Providence. Betsey Williams gave the land to the city. She was Roger Williams' great-great-great-granddaughter. The Betsey Williams Cottage is in the park. So is the Roger Williams Zoo. It has polar bears, penguins, giraffes, and elephants. The Museum of Natural History is also in the park. It has displays on the people and wildlife of Narragansett Bay.

Downtown Providence

Polar bears at the Roger Williams Zoo

Many homes from the 1700s line Providence's hilly streets. One of them is the Governor Stephen Hopkins House. Hopkins governed colonial Rhode Island for ten years. George Washington visited his

33

John and Joseph Brown were brothers. They belonged to a wealthy Providence merchant family. Other family members were their brothers Nicholas and Moses.

Brown University

house twice. The John Brown House was built by Joseph Brown in 1786. It is a beautiful three-story home. John Brown's chariot can be seen at the carriage house. George Washington rode in it when he visited Providence.

Providence has many great schools, too. Brown University is there. It was begun in 1764. Brown is one of the country's oldest and finest colleges. Nicholas Brown gave much money to start the school. The University of Rhode Island has a Providence branch. Rhode Island School of Design is also in Providence. This school runs the Museum of Art. American and French paintings are on view there. Young visitors like the museum's Egyptian mummy.

Providence is also the state capital. State lawmakers meet in the State House. The *Independent Man* stands atop the building's huge dome. This statue stands for Rhode Islanders' freedom to follow their beliefs. Inside the State House is a portrait of George Washington. It was painted by Rhode Island artist Gilbert Stuart.

NORTHERN RHODE ISLAND HIGHLIGHTS

Cranston is just south of Providence. It was settled around 1638. The town was named for Samuel

Cranston. He governed Rhode Island for twenty-nine years. That was longer than anyone else. Today, Cranston has about 76,000 people. It is Rhode Island's third-biggest city. The Governor Sprague Mansion is in Cranston. Two Rhode Island governors named William Sprague were born there. They were uncle and nephew. The Sprague Mansion shows how wealthy people lived in the 1800s. Cranston's Joy Homestead shows how plainer people lived. Job Joy was a farmer and shoemaker. He built his farmhouse around 1778.

Elected at age twenty-nine, the second William Sprague was Rhode Island's youngest governor.

The State House

Warwick is south of Cranston. It was settled in 1643. Today, Warwick is Rhode Island's second-biggest city. More than 85,000 people live there. The Warwick Museum displays works by Rhode Island artists. Warwick also has the country's first state-owned airport. T. F. Green State Airport opened in 1931. Near Warwick is Coventry. The General Nathanael Greene Homestead is there. Visitors can see his writing desk and drinking mug.

Pawtucket is north of Providence. With about 73,000 people, Pawtucket is Rhode Island's fourth-

The Slater Mill Historic Site, in Pawtucket

largest city. Slater Mill Historic Site is at Pawtucket. The Slater Mill is known as the "Cradle of American Industry." It helped establish the country's cloth-making business. The mill also helped start the machine age in United States factories. The Children's Museum of Rhode Island is another Pawtucket highlight. It has a giant map of Rhode Island. The map nearly fills the floor of one room.

Woonsocket is near Rhode Island's northeast corner. It's the state's sixth-largest city. Many people who live there have a French-Canadian background. Woonsocket has a historic City Hall. Abraham Lincoln spoke there in 1860. He was running for president. Smithfield is south of Woonsocket. Powder Mill Ledges Wildlife Refuge is there. Visitors see deer, woodchucks, and turtles. Red-tailed hawks fly overhead. Chickadees and owls also live there.

To the west is Chepachet. Its Brown & Hopkins Country Store dates from 1809. Everything from penny candy to antiques is sold there. This is the country's oldest continuously running country store.

To the south is Foster. The Town House in Foster dates from 1796. It is the country's oldest town house. People still gather there for town meetings. They discuss the town's business.

Pawtucket is an Indian *name meaning "place by the waterfall."*

The Children's Museum of Rhode Island has a huge relief map of the state.

Southern Rhode Island Highlights

Fisherville Brook Wildlife Refuge is in Exeter. Otters, beavers, great blue herons, and wood ducks live there. Male wood ducks are the country's most colorful ducks. They are purple, blue, green, red, white, and yellow.

Kingston is south of the refuge. It's home to the University of Rhode Island's main campus. This is the state's biggest school. It has about 15,000 students. This is about twice as many people as live in Kingston. South of Kingston is Charlestown. The Narragansetts' headquarters is there. Each year, they hold a thanksgiving festival. Dancing, crafts, and foods are part of the fun.

Narragansett is to the south on the coast. Whale-watching cruises leave from the town each summer day. People can see finback, humpback, and sperm whales. Across the state to the west is Hopkinton. The Enchanted Forest is there. This is a popular amusement park. Children can enter the House that Jack Built. They can board the Pirate Ship.

Westerly is farther south. The Babcock-Smith House is there. Dr. Joshua Babcock lived in it. He was Westerly's first doctor. He was also a judge in the 1700s. Benjamin Franklin often visited Babcock.

Franklin invented the lightning rod. He placed these rods on Babcock's house. They protected the house from lightning.

Watch Hill is in the far southwest corner of Rhode Island. Visitors enjoy its sandy beaches. The Flying Horse Carousel is in Watch Hill. It dates from about 1867. This is one of the country's oldest merry-go-rounds. Real horses once turned it.

THE ISLANDS OF RHODE ISLAND

Block Island is in the Atlantic Ocean. It's 12 miles offshore. People reach Block Island by ferries or air-

These huge, beautiful homes can be seen in Watch Hill.

39

Jamestown Windmill (left) and Beaver Tail Lighthouse (right) are Conanicut Island landmarks.

planes. More than forty rare plants and animals are found there. Visitors can view the sea from Mohegan Bluffs. The bluffs stand 185 feet above the ocean.

Conanicut Island is in Narragansett Bay. Pirate William Kidd was said to have buried treasure there. Jamestown is Conanicut's only town. Jamestown Windmill is on the island. It was built in 1787. The windmill has been fixed to grind grain once again. The island's Beaver Tail Lighthouse was built in

1856. Nearby are the remains of an earlier lighthouse. That one was built in 1749.

To the east is Aquidneck Island. Newport is on the island's south end. Old Colony House was built in 1739. It served as one of Rhode Island's capitols until 1900. It is one of the country's oldest capitol buildings. Touro Synagogue is another Newport landmark. It was completed in 1763. That makes it the country's oldest Jewish house of worship.

Today, about 28,000 people live in Newport. The town is known for its huge, beautiful homes.

Touro Synagogue

Visitors can see many Newport mansions from the Cliff Walk. This 3-mile trail goes past the Breakers, Marble House, and Rosecliff.

Newport is also well known for its sailing races. One of them is the Newport-to-Bermuda Race. Each year, the city hosts the Hall of Fame Tennis Championships. The International Tennis Hall of Fame is in Newport. Newport is known for music, too. Many visitors attend the Newport Music Festival. They also come for the Newport Jazz Festival.

Portsmouth lies on the north end of Aquidneck Island. Green Animals Topiary Gardens is there. It has eighty specially cut shrubs. They are shaped like animals such as giraffes and camels.

EAST BAY

Eastern Rhode Island is called East Bay. Its land stretches from Massachusetts into Narragansett Bay. Bristol lies in northern East Bay. It is home to Blithewold Mansion and Gardens. The mansion has forty-five rooms. Thousands of flowers help make this estate beautiful. The Haffenreffer Museum is also in Bristol. It has special exhibits on American Indians. Visitors also learn about people from Africa, Asia, and the Pacific.

Green Animals Topiary Gardens, in Portsmouth

Bristol is also home to the Herreshoff Marine Museum. Boats made by the Herreshoff Manufacturing Company can be seen there. One is a 20-foot catboat. It was built in 1859 by John and Nathanael Herreshoff. The brothers were seventeen and eleven at the time.

To the south is Tiverton. The Ruecker Wildlife Refuge is there. Visitors can spot herons, egrets, and ospreys. Close to Rhode Island's southeastern tip is Little Compton. The Rhode Island Red Monument stands there. This chicken was first bred at Little Compton in the 1850s.

Rosecliff is one of Newport's many mansions.

Overleaf: Roger Williams

43

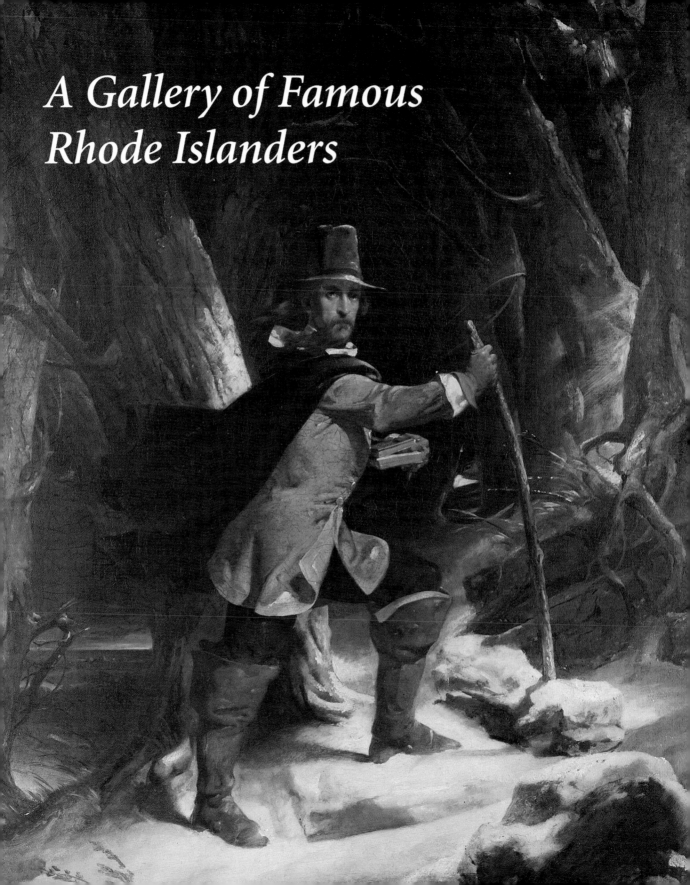

A Gallery of Famous
Rhode Islanders

A Gallery of Famous Rhode Islanders

Rhode Island produced several Indian and colonial leaders. Other well-known Rhode Islanders became sailors and built boats. Still others became great artists, authors, songwriters, and singers.

Massasoit (1580?-1661) was chief of the Wampanoags of Rhode Island and Massachusetts. He befriended the Massachusetts Pilgrims. He sold land in Rhode Island to Roger Williams. One of Massasoit's sons was **Metacomet** (1639?-1676). He was born near present-day Bristol. Metacomet became Wampanoag chief in 1663. He hated the colonists for taking Indian lands. The colonists called him King Philip. In 1675-76, Metacomet fought for his people's lands. This was called King Philip's War. He was killed near Mt. Hope by an enemy Indian.

Weatamoo (1650?-1676) was born near Rhode Island's eastern border with Massachusetts. She was a great fighter. Weatamoo became the chief of the Pocassets, a small tribe that lived around Tiverton. Weatamoo led 300 warriors in King Philip's War. She, too, was killed during the fighting.

Chief Metacomet

45

Roger Williams (1603?-1683) was born in England. He was a minister there. In 1631, Williams moved to Massachusetts. He thought that church and government should be separate. This got him into trouble. Williams then founded the colony of Rhode Island. People of all faiths were welcome there. Williams also treated the Indians fairly. One of his books was about Indian languages.

Left: Anne Hutchinson
Right: Matthew C. Perry

Anne Hutchinson (1591-1643) was born in England. At the age of forty-three, she sailed to

Boston. Hutchinson became a town leader. She nursed the sick and helped deliver babies. Hutchinson had fifteen children of her own. She also led church meetings. Hutchinson taught that God was loving, not cruel. For that, she was forced out of Massachusetts. Hutchinson traveled 65 miles by foot and canoe. She arrived at Aquidneck Island. There, Hutchinson helped found Portsmouth.

Nathanael Greene (1742-1786) was born near Warwick. In his youth, he made little anchors and other toys. He sold these to buy books. Greene became a great Revolutionary War general.

Some well-known sailors came from Rhode Island. **Esek Hopkins** (1718-1802) was born in present-day Scituate. He led the U.S. Navy during the Revolutionary War. Hopkins defeated the British in the Bahamas. **Robert Gray** (1755-1806) was born in Tiverton. In 1790, he became the first American to sail around the world. In 1792, Gray discovered the Columbia River. This is in the American Northwest. He named the river for his ship.

Oliver Hazard Perry (1785-1819) was born in South Kingstown. During the War of 1812, he won the Battle of Lake Erie. Afterward, he sent this message: "We have met the enemy and they are ours." **Matthew Calbraith Perry** (1794-1858) was Oli-

Esek Hopkins

*Left: John B.
Herreshoff
Right: Ida Lewis*

ver's brother. Matthew was born in Newport. He led
American ships to Japan in 1853. This opened trade
between Japan and the United States.

Isaac Touro (1738-1783) was a Jewish leader.
He came to Newport from Jamaica in 1760. He led
the first service at Newport's Touro Synagogue
(1763). His son, **Judah Touro** (1775-1854), was
born in Newport. Judah became a rich merchant in
New Orleans. There, he fought for the United
States in the War of 1812. Judah suffered a terrible
leg wound. Judah Touro left more than $500 mil-
lion to charities around the world.

Prudence Crandall (1803-1890) was born in Hopkinton. She opened a girls' school in Connecticut in 1831. Later, she admitted a black girl. Many people objected. So Crandall planned to start a school for black girls. She was then put in jail. Crandall is remembered as an early fighter for the rights of black people.

John Brown Herreshoff (1841-1915) was born near Bristol. At age fourteen, he lost his sight. In 1863, he and his brother **Nathanael Herreshoff** (1848-1938) formed the Herreshoff Manufacturing Company. The brothers built hundreds of sailing vessels. Among them were America's Cup winners *Vigilant* and *Columbia*.

Ida Lewis (1842?-1911) was born in Newport. Her father was lighthouse keeper at Newport Harbor. Lewis took over his work when her father became ill. At about age sixteen, she rescued four men. Their boat had overturned. Lewis later saved many other lives. Her last rescue was in 1904. Lewis was at least sixty years old then.

Gilbert Stuart (1755-1828) was born in North Kingstown. As a child, he drew pictures of people. Stuart became a great portrait artist. His paintings of George Washington are well known. **Nancy Elizabeth Prophet** (1890-1960) was born in Warwick.

Gilbert Stuart

She was part Narragansett Indian and part African-American. Prophet was a great sculptor. *Silence* is one of her best works. It's a woman's head carved from marble.

H. P. Lovecraft (1890-1937) was born in Providence. He wrote scary stories. One of them is "The Dreams in the Witch-House." Another is "The Thing on the Doorstep." **Edwin O'Connor** (1918-1968) was also born in Providence. He grew up in Woonsocket. O'Connor was a radio announcer. Then he won fame as an author. *The Last Hurrah* is a well-known O'Connor novel. *The Edge of Sadness* won him the 1962 Pulitzer Prize in fiction. **Natalie Babbitt** was born in Ohio in 1932. Later, she settled in Providence. Babbitt is a well-known children's author and illustrator. Her books include *Tuck Everlasting* and *Nellie—A Cat on Her Own.*

Author Avi Wortis, known simply as **Avi,** has lived in Providence since 1987. The New York native was born in 1937. Avi always wanted to be a writer. His books are full of suspense. Avi's first book of stories, *Things That Sometimes Happen,* was written for his young sons. *The Man Who Was Poe* and *Something Upstairs: A Tale of Ghosts* were set in colonial and modern Providence. *The True Confessions of Charlotte Doyle* was a Newbery Honor Book.

George M. Cohan (1878-1942) was born in Providence. As a boy, he played the violin in a hometown theater. Cohan became a songwriter. He wrote "Over There." This was a well-known World War I tune. "I'm a Yankee Doodle Dandy" is another Cohan song. **Nelson Eddy** (1901-1967) was also born in Providence. As a boy, he sang in his church choir. Eddy became a singing film star. Two of his best-known films are *Rose Marie* and *Sweethearts*.

Three Baseball Hall of Famers were born in Rhode Island. Outfielder **Hugh Duffy** (1866-1954) was born in River Point. Duffy hit .438 in 1894. This was the highest average in National

Cohan's life story was told in the movie Yankee Doodle Dandy.

Left: George M. Cohan Right: Nelson Eddy with Jeanette MacDonald in the movie Rose Marie.

League history. Second baseman **Napoleon "Nap" Lajoie** (1875-1959) was born in Woonsocket. He had the highest American League average ever. In 1901, Lajoie hit .422. **Charles "Gabby" Hartnett** (1900-1972) was also born in Woonsocket. He was a great catcher. Hartnett drove in 1,179 runs in his career.

Glenna Collett Vare (1903-1989) was born in Providence. At the age of thirteen, she went to the Metacomet Golf Course. Her father had Vare hit a few balls. Later, she became a great golfer. Vare won six U.S. Women's Amateur Championships. She was still playing at the age of eighty-three.

"Gabby" Hartnett

The birthplace of Nathanael Greene, Prudence Crandall, Napoleon Lajoie, and Nancy Elizabeth Prophet . . .

Home, too, of Massasoit, Roger Williams, Anne Hutchinson, Natalie Babbitt, and Isaac Touro . . .

The birthplace of religious freedom in America, the Cradle of American Industry, and the first state to declare its independence from England . . .

A state well known for its sailing races and music festivals, and for making jewelry and silverware . . .

This is the Ocean State—Rhode Island!

Glenna Collett Vare (left) being given one of her many golf trophies

Did You Know?

In 1762, Ann Franklin of the Newport *Mercury* became one of the country's first female newspaper editors. She was related by marriage to Benjamin Franklin.

A Gilbert Stuart portrait of George Washington is shown on United States one-dollar bills.

General Ambrose Burnside of Rhode Island grew whiskers beneath his ears. They were called *burnsides*. The name was later changed to *sideburns*.

From 1854 to 1900, Rhode Island's capital was shared between Providence and Newport. In 1900, Providence became the only permanent capital.

Before becoming a New York Yankees star, Babe Ruth played for the Providence Grays in 1914.

Dime, Dollar, and Cent streets in Providence reflect the city's banking heritage.

FEDERAL RESERVE NOTE

UNITED STATES OF AMERICA

IS LEGAL TENDER
PUBLIC AND PRIVATE

D 00846451 A

WASHINGTON, D.C.

1

4

The country's first auto race on a track was held at Cranston in 1896. The cars went only about 25 miles per hour.

Bristol claims to hold the country's oldest Fourth of July parade. The tradition dates back to the 1780s.

Our smallest state has the longest official name—*State of Rhode Island and Providence Plantations.*

Sarah Sands was one of America's first female doctors. Dr. Sands practiced on Block Island. She died there in 1702.

Rhode Island has islands named Hope, Prudence, and Patience. The state has villages named Hope, Harmony, and Liberty.

The country's first public roller-skating rink opened in Newport in 1866.

The Old Stone Mill is in Newport. Most historians think this round tower dates from the 1600s. But some people insist it was built by Vikings around the year 1000.

RHODE ISLAND INFORMATION

State flag

Violets

Area: 1,212 square miles (the smallest of the fifty states)

Greatest Distance North to South: 48 miles

Greatest Distance East to West: 37 miles

Coastline: 40 miles of general coastline; 384 miles of coastline counting all bays and islands

Borders: Massachusetts to the east and north; Connecticut to the west; the Atlantic Ocean to the south

Highest Point: Jerimoth Hill in the northwest, 812 feet above sea level

Lowest Point: Sea level, along the seashore

Hottest Recorded Temperature: 104° F. (at Providence, on August 2, 1975)

Coldest Recorded Temperature: -23° F. (at Kingston, on January 11, 1942)

Statehood: The thirteenth state, on May 29, 1790

Origin of Name: Some say *Rhode Island* came from explorer Giovanni da Verrazano who thought a nearby island looked like the island of Rhodes near Greece; others say Dutch explorer Adriaen Block named a nearby island *Roodt Eylandt*—Dutch words meaning "Red Island"—after that island's red clay shore

Capital: Providence

Counties: 5

United States Senators: 2

United States Representatives: 2

State Senators: 50

State Representatives: 100

State Song: "Rhode Island," by T. Clarke Brown

State Motto: "Hope"

Nicknames: "Ocean State," "Little Rhody"

State Seal: Adopted in 1896

State Flag: Adopted in 1897

State Colors: Blue, white, and gold

State Flower: Violet

State Bird: Rhode Island Red

State Tree: Red maple

State Shell: Quahog

Some Islands: Aquidneck, Block, Despair, Conanicut, Prudence

Some Rivers: Blackstone, Woonasquatucket, Chepachet, Pawtuxet, Wood, Queen

Some Lakes and Ponds: Scituate, Wilson, Pascoag, Watchaug, Worden

Wildlife: White-tailed deer, foxes, woodchucks, rabbits, minks, raccoons, turtles, gulls, loons, ducks, pheasants, owls, blue jays, hawks, chickadees, mockingbirds, bluebirds, great blue herons, egrets, kingfishers, ospreys, many other kinds of birds, whales, bass, pickerels, trout, bluefish, flounder, swordfish, tuna, many other kinds of fish

Fishing Products: Lobster, oysters, clams, flounder, cod, tuna, swordfish

Mining Products: Crushed stone, sand and gravel

Farm Products: Sod, trees, shrubs, other nursery plants, milk, potatoes, apples, hay, chickens, turkeys, eggs

Manufactured Products: Jewelry, silverware, nuts, bolts, wires, other metal goods, boats, ships, machine tools, newsprint, stationery, medical instruments, clothing, chemicals, foods, toys

Population: 1,003,464, forty-third among the states (1990 U.S. Census Bureau figures)

Major Cities (1990 Census):

Providence	160,728	East Providence	50,380
Warwick	85,427	Woonsocket	43,877
Cranston	76,060	Newport	28,227
Pawtucket	72,644	Central Falls	17,637

Rhode Island Red

Red maple leaves
Red maple tree

Rhode Island History

About 6000 B.C.—The first people reach Rhode Island

About A.D. 1000—Vikings may have reached Rhode Island

1524—Giovanni da Verrazano, an Italian sailing for the French, explores Rhode Island's Narragansett Bay

Early 1600s—Rhode Island is home to roughly 10,000 American Indians, about half of them Narragansetts

1614—Dutch explorer Adriaen Block reaches Rhode Island

1635—William Blackstone becomes Rhode Island's first settler

1636—Roger Williams begins Providence

1638—Anne Hutchinson and others found Portsmouth

1639—Newport is begun

1642—Warwick is founded

1644—Roger Williams receives a charter from England to unite the four towns as the Rhode Island Colony

1675-76—King Philip's War ends in an Indian defeat in southern Rhode Island

1732—The *Rhode Island Gazette,* the colony's first newspaper, is published at Newport

1769—Patriots burn the English ship *Liberty* at Newport

1772—Patriots burn the English ship *Gaspee* near Providence

1774—Rhode Island is the first of the thirteen colonies to outlaw the importing of slaves

1775-83—The Revolutionary War is fought; about 10,000 Rhode Islanders help the United States win its independence

1776—On May 4, Rhode Island is the first colony to drop its allegiance to the King of England

1778—The Battle of Rhode Island ends in a draw

1790—On May 29, Rhode Island becomes the thirteenth state; at Pawtucket, Samuel Slater sets up the country's first water-powered machines for making cotton yarn

Adriaen Block building a boat with his men

1835—The state's first railroad is established between Providence and Boston

1842—In June, the "Dorr Rebellion" for more voting rights is put down; in November, a new constitution, allowing more people to vote, is adopted

1854—Rhode Island Red chickens are first bred at Little Compton

1861-65—The Civil War is fought between the northern and southern states

1890—Happy 100th birthday, state of Rhode Island!

1892—The University of Rhode Island is founded

1900—Providence becomes the permanent capital

1917-18—Rhode Island sends ships and 28,000 troops to help win World War I

1920s—Many textile companies leave Rhode Island and move to the South

1929-39—The Great Depression causes banks, factories, and mines around the country to close and farmers to lose their land

1938—Rhode Island is the state hardest hit by the New England Hurricane

1941-45—Rhode Island provides 100,000 men and women, plus vessels and torpedoes to help win World War II

1969—The Newport Bridge is finished

1978—An agreement is made to return some land to the Narragansett Indians

1986—Rhode Island celebrates Providence's 350th birthday

1989—A big oil spill occurs in Narragansett Bay

1990—Rhode Island suffers a banking crisis and a money shortage for state government operations; Rhode Island celebrates its 200th birthday

1991—Hurricane Bob causes about $115 million in property damage

MAP KEY

GLOSSARY

antislavery: Against slavery

capital: A city that is the seat of government

capitol: The building in which the government meets

climate: The typical weather of a place

coast: The land along a large body of water

colony: A settlement outside a parent country but ruled by the parent country

constitution: A framework of government

explorer: A person who visits and studies unknown lands

glacier: A mass of slowly moving ice

hurricane: A huge windstorm that forms over the ocean

independence: Freedom to act and live on one's own

industry: A large business activity

manufacturing: The making of products

merchant: A person who buys and sells goods

million: A thousand thousand (1,000,000)

monument: A building or statue that honors a person, thing, or important event

permanent: Lasting

pollution: The harming of the environment

population: The number of people in a place

portrait: A picture of a person

reservoir: A man-made lake where water is stored

sculptor: A person who makes statues and other three-dimensional artworks

slave: A person who is owned by another person

textile: Cloth, or thread to make cloth

town meeting: A meeting at which the people of a town choose officials and decide other local matters

transportation: The moving of people and goods

wildlife refuge: A place where wild animals are protected

Southeast Light on Mohegan Bluffs, Block Island

PICTURE ACKNOWLEDGMENTS

Front cover, ©Michael Carroll/**NE Stock Photo**; 1, ©George Glod/**SuperStock**; 2, **Tom Dunnington**; 3, **©Paul A. Darling**; 5, **Tom Dunnington**; 6-7, **©Tom Till**; 8, ©Michael Giannacio/**NE Stock Photo**; 9, **Courtesy of Hammond Incorporated, Maplewood, New Jersey**; 10 (left), ©Skip Moody/**Dembinsky Photo Assoc.**; 10 (right), **©North Wind Pictures**; 11, ©Clyde H. Smith/**NE Stock Photo**; 12, **©Paul A. Darling**; 15, **The Bettmann Archive**; 16, ©John Wells/**NE Stock Photo**; 17, **©North Wind Pictures, hand-colored**; 18, 19, **The Rhode Island Historical Society**; 20, **Slater Mill Historic Site**; 21, 22, 23, **The Rhode Island Historical Society**; 25, ©Jim Schwabel/**NE Stock Photo**; 26, **©Paul A. Darling**; 27, **©Mary Ann Brockman**; 28 (both pictures), **©Paul A. Darling**; 29, ©George Jacobs/**SuperStock**; 30-31, ©Jim Schwabel/**NE Stock Photo**; 32, ©Andre Jenny/**NE Stock Photo**; 33 (top), ©R. Kord/**H. Armstrong Roberts**; 33 (bottom), ©Jim Schwabel/**NE Stock Photo**; 34, **©Paul A. Darling**; 35, ©Andre Jenny/**NE Stock Photo**; 36, ©Clyde H. Smith/**NE Stock Photo**; 37, **©Paul A. Darling**; 39, ©Jim Schwabel/**NE Stock Photo**; 40 (left), ©Chuck Schmeiser/**NE Stock Photo**; 40 (right), ©Jim Schwabel/**NE Stock Photo**; 41, ©Howard Karger/**NE Stock Photo**; 42, ©Jim Schwabel/**NE Stock Photo**; 43, ©John Clark/**Photri, Inc.**; 44, 45, 46 (right), **The Rhode Island Historical Society**; 46 (left), **Stock Montage, Inc.**; 47, **The Bettmann Archive**; 48 (both pictures), **The Rhode Island Historical Society**; 49, **The Bettmann Archive**; 51 (left), **UPI/Bettmann**; 51 (right), 52, 53, **AP/Wide World Photos**; 54 (top), **UPI/Bettmann**; 55 (top), **The Rhode Island Historical Society**; 55 (bottom), **©Paul A. Darling**; 56 (top), **Courtesy Flag Research Center, Winchester, Massachusetts 01890**; 56 (bottom), ©Kitty Kohout/**Root Resources**; 57 (top), ©Rod Planck/**Dembinsky Photo Assoc.**; 57 (middle), ©Bill Lea/**Dembinsky Photo Assoc.**; 57 (bottom), ©Ron Goulet/**Dembinsky Photo Assoc.**; 58, **North Wind Picture Archives, hand-colored**; 60, **Tom Dunnington**; 62, **©Tom Till**; back cover, ©David Forbert/**SuperStock**

INDEX

Page numbers in boldface type indicate illustrations.

ABOUT THE AUTHORS

Dennis and Judith Fradin have coauthored several books in the From Sea to Shining Sea series. The Fradins both graduated from Northwestern University in 1967. Dennis has been a professional writer for twenty years, and has published 150 books. His works for Childrens Press include the Young People's Stories of Our States series, the Disaster! series, and the Thirteen Colonies series. Judith earned her M.A. in literature from Northwestern University and taught high-school and college English for many years. The Fradins, who are the parents of Anthony, Diana, and Michael, live in Evanston, Illinois.

BOSTON PUBLIC LIBRARY

3 9999 03077 663 5

CODMAN SQUARE